Spot the Differences

Lizard or Salamander?

by Jamie Rice

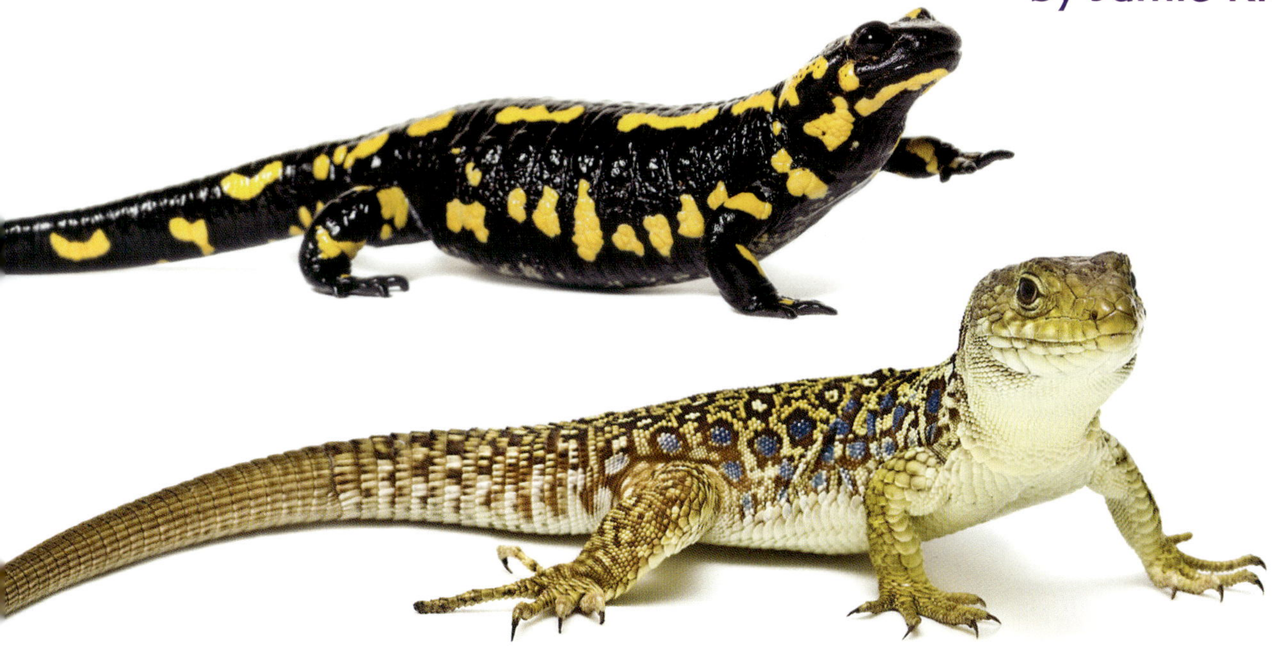

Ideas for Parents and Teachers

Bullfrog Books let children practice reading informational text at the earliest reading levels. Repetition, familiar words, and photo labels support early readers.

Before Reading

- Discuss the cover photo. What does it tell them?
- Look at the picture glossary together. Read and discuss the words.

Read the Book

- "Walk" through the book and look at the photos. Let the child ask questions. Point out the photo labels.
- Read the book to the child, or have him or her read independently.

After Reading

- Prompt the child to think more. Ask: What did you know about lizards and salamanders before reading this book? What more would you like to learn?

Bullfrog Books are published by Jump!
5357 Penn Avenue South
Minneapolis, MN 55419
www.jumplibrary.com

Library of Congress Cataloging-in-Publication Data

Names: Rice, Jamie, author.
Title: Lizard or salamander? / by Jamie Rice.
Description: Minneapolis, MN: Jump!, Inc., [2023]
Series: Spot the differences | Includes index.
Audience: Ages 5–8
Identifiers: LCCN 2022011675 (print)
LCCN 2022011676 (ebook)
ISBN 9798885241700 (hardcover)
ISBN 9798885241717 (paperback)
ISBN 9798885241724 (ebook)
Subjects: LCSH: Lizards—Juvenile literature.
Salamanders—Juvenile literature.
Classification: LCC QL666.L2 R53 2023 (print)
LCC QL666.L2 (ebook) | DDC 597.8/5—dc23/eng/20220413
LC record available at https://lccn.loc.gov/2022011675
LC ebook record available at https://lccn.loc.gov/2022011676

Editor: Katie Chanez
Designer: Emma Bersie

Photo Credits: PetlinDmitry/Shutterstock, cover (left); James DeBoer/Shutterstock, cover (right); Eric Isselee/Shutterstock, 1 (top), 24 (top); Angel Luis Simon Martin/Dreamstime, 1 (bottom); WildMedia/Shutterstock, 3, 16–17, 23tl; Jason Bazzano/Alamy, 4; Dan_Koleska/Shutterstock, 5; BOONCHUAY PROMJIAM/Shutterstock, 6–7 (top); Tomas Hilger/Shutterstock, 6–7 (bottom); Nathan A Shepard/Shutterstock, 8–9, 23br; Norjipin Saidi/Shutterstock, 10–11, 23tr; Design Pics Inc/Alamy, 12–13; Sholmes370/Shutterstock, 14–15; Frank Lane Picture Agency/SuperStock, 18–19; Paulo Ragner/Shutterstock, 20; Gerald A. DeBoer/Shutterstock, 21, 23bl; medvezok/Shutterstock, 22 (left); JaklZdenek/Shutterstock, 22 (right); Will Thomass/Shutterstock, 24 (bottom).

Printed in the United States of America at Corporate Graphics in North Mankato, Minnesota.

Table of Contents

How to Use This Book

In this book, you will see pictures of both lizards and salamanders. Can you tell which one is in each picture?

Hint: You can find the answers if you flip the book upside down!

How Many Toes?

This is a lizard.

This is a salamander.

They look the same.

But they are not.

How?

Let's see!

A lizard's skin is dry.
It is rough.
A salamander's is wet.
It is smooth.
Which is this?

Answer: salamander

Both have ears.

We can see a lizard's.

We can't see a salamander's.

Which is this?

Answer: lizard

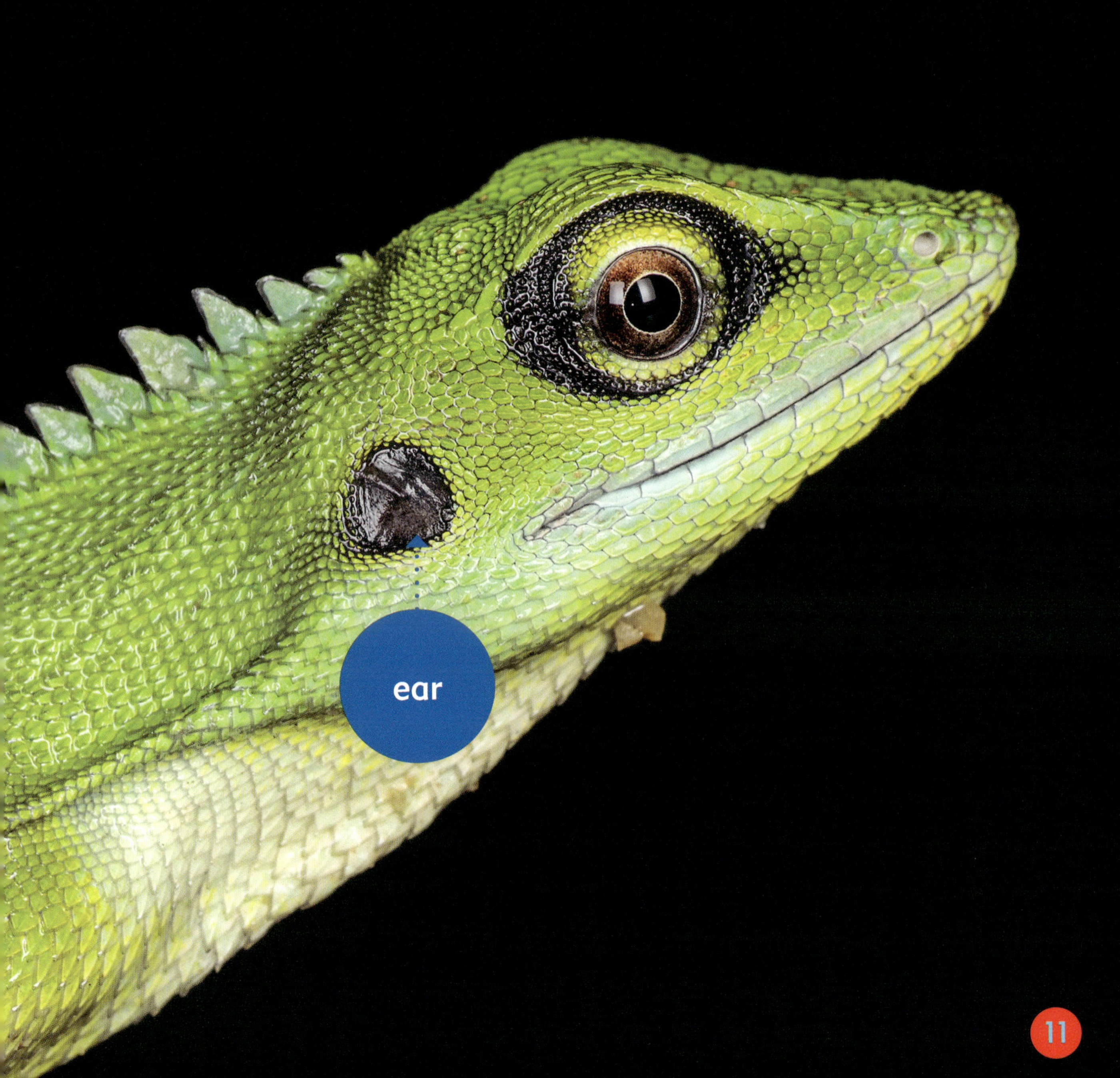
ear

toe

Both have toes.

A lizard has
five front toes.

A salamander
has four.

Which is this?

Answer: salamander

Do you see claws?

A lizard has them.

A salamander does not.

Which is this?

Answer: lizard

A lizard stays on land.

It stays dry.

A salamander goes in water.

It stays wet.

Which is this?

Answer: lizard

A lizard lays eggs in dirt.

A salamander lays eggs in water.

Who laid these?

Answer: salamander

eggs

See and Compare

Lizard

Salamander

long tail
smooth skin
shorter legs
five back toes
four front toes

Quick Facts

Lizards and salamanders have long tails. Their bodies are similar shapes. Both lay eggs. They are similar, but they have differences. Take a look!

Lizards

- are reptiles
- live on land
- lay eggs in dirt or sand
- are more active during the day
- sit in the sun to stay warm

Salamanders

- are amphibians
- live both on land and in water
- lay eggs in water
- are more active at night
- go in water to stay wet

Picture Glossary

dry
Not wet.

rough
Having a surface with many bumps.

smooth
Having an even surface without bumps.

wet
Not dry, or still damp.

Index

To Learn More

Finding more information is as easy as 1, 2, 3.

1. Go to www.factsurfer.com
2. Enter "lizardorsalamander?" into the search box.
3. Choose your book to see a list of websites.